A Leader's Field Guide:

From someone who hates leadership books

Author
Trevin Hermosillo

INTRODUCTION

Hello Reader,

Imagine that we're catching a drink together at the bar. Or sitting on the tailgate shooting the shit. This whole book is informal. I'm going to talk to you like I would talk to a close friend. We have come to the table as equals. You may not agree with some of the things I have to say. That's ok. Let's agree to disagree.

In my early 20s, I spent ten years working for a large railroad company. Spending most of that time somehow involved in the safety program. I was a traveling mechanic type of safety guy. This meant traveling around and meeting with other mechanics. I would do routine building and truck audits. Plus, I lead yearly meetings of 200 plus people as well as taught Smith system driving, behavior-based safety and any other presentation someone decided they could throw into a PowerPoint.

Later on in my career, I taught rules. Manager of Field Training. Fancy title, un-fancy job.

Just like any Fortune 500 company, you can imagine there's a lot of management involved. Managers overseeing other managers, who in turn manage more managers.

Management is all about leadership and would actually froth at the mouth and become erect if you asked to go to any kind of training or if you were reading a leadership or self-help book. It was a quick way to ensure you would get that nod of approval, the slap on the back or, most importantly, an exceeds on your yearly report. Exceeds would get you 100% of your bonus.

I would fly all over the country, and during that time, it was an easy thing for me to read. I consumed all of the leadership books I could get my hands on. Hoping that there would be some piece of information that I hadn't heard before. Some revolutionary bit of wisdom that would all of a sudden make my life easier. I mean, the bigwigs had to have known it, right? The secret that allowed them to keep getting promoted. We all know pay grade in the company is solely based on how many self-help and leadership books you've read. We also know that reading a book and then being able to brag about it later makes you really smart. "Bill Gates didn't finish college, but I'm sure he read this book I'm reading; therefore, I'm smart, and you're dumb." If you're in management, then you know that it only gets worse the higher you go.

I'm a fairly quick reader. I could crank through a book on a couple-hour flight with no problem. The only issue here is that I needed to read more. I had to feed the monster. I poured through every airport bookstore and found nothing but the same old recycled bullshit that someone had worded differently, hoping to make a buck. It infuriated me. It still infuriates me. I think that the self-help section rarely helps you; it helps pad the pocket of the author who wrote it. Who do these people think they are that are writing all of these? Who thinks they have the answers?
Don't get me wrong; like everything, there are exceptions to the rule.

(I gaze upon myself in the mirror and realize I have become what I've despised the most as I am typing this now. A monster.)

I went to seminars, clinics, and workshops. I even joined a book club. Yes, I stooped so low as to join a company book club. It had to be out there. That piece of knowledge the upper echelon claimed to have. If I could unlock it, then a light would beam down upon me, and I would ascend into the heavens, not only growing a double chin but also transforming into something akin to Jabba the Hutt, becoming an ever-powerful supervisor. This would then allow me to get that huge pay raise they dangled like a carrot. At least that's what they wanted us to believe.

I'm sure one of the bigwigs said this to me,
"Just a few more books, kid, just a few more classes, and you can have a job like me. Did I mention that my bonus comes in cash that I have to haul out using a wheelbarrow?"

My eyes flashed dollar signs, and I was even more motivated to figure out this secret.

I then took some public speaking classes, which turned into becoming a master speaker whatever that means.
I became the judge who judged everyone else's speaking.

(By the way, come a little closer, closer, I'm whispering now. I think that all you need to be a public speaker is confidence. The rest comes later.)

Anyway, it never happened. What did happen is I became jaded and frustrated.
It doesn't seem that deep.
Does it?

I eventually quit and started my own business, which led to several business ventures. This led to managing managers that each had their own team and setting them up for success. This led to a snowball effect and allowed me to sit at the table with CEO's and decision-makers. It didn't take long to see how these guys were leading their people. Everyone is different, that's for sure.
Ok, I digress. Let's move on.

I am a jack-of-all-trades, but I do one thing really well. I am an effective communicator. I have focused on honing in on that skill. I would say I even specialize in effective communication. So it may not be a surprise that a byproduct of that is being able to lead effectively just because of effective communication.

If you would like to stop reading now, you have 50% of the secret sauce to leadership. If you're being forced to read this to impress your boss, just make your whole speech about effective communication and complain about how dry this book was. Say you didn't agree with the non-contingent reinforcement part and finish by shouting the word "INTEGRITY", and you should be good to go.

Now, earlier, I said that it infuriates me to see people write a leadership book and have all of these steps, keys, and things you need, but I really feel like it's simple. I'm going to try to break it down into the rawest form in this book. This is really just an answer to everything I've read. My goal is to provide a layman's terms guide of what has worked for me and when you strip down all the fancy words of what leadership is. I get going on the topic and can't shut up, so the easiest thing I could come up with was to throw all the information I have on the wall like spaghetti and let you, the humble reader, take any little nugget of information that may help you. Take a piece, take it all.

I've broken things down into categories, so just hang in there. Bend the ears of the book, highlight it, tear out pages. I spent a lot of time thinking about how long this book should even be. They say you need so many words to qualify as a book, and I'm far below the mark. Then it dawns on me. All this fluff I read and all the bullshit could just be because the writer was focused on the word count to get a publisher to make sales. This is a guide; guides are short.
 Heck, use this book as a leadership tool by slapping your employee or boss with it if all else fails.
(please don't do that. I'm not sure if I could get into trouble for instructing that.)

Ok, ok, I don't hate leadership books. It was a catchy title, and it got you this far….. I dislike them.

Unfortunately, leadership is not something everyone has. Hell, I don't feel like I have it. Maybe that's a characteristic of a leader. I do know that, for some reason, people listen when I speak and feel comfortable sharing things with me, and well, I guess that's a part of leadership, right?
Can it be taught? I think so.
Is a true leader born that way?
I think that it's more likely true. It's a question I've been asking for years. I think leadership can be taught, and I think some have to work harder than others to get there, but it can be done. They have to want

to. You have to want to. It's not something that can just be forced, or a magic formula followed. It's hard work and introspection.

Trait theory suggests that you need to be born with certain traits to be a leader. I agree just as I agree that to be an Iron Man triathlon competitor, you need to be born with certain traits, but with enough willpower and drive, you can train and compete. You may not come in 1st, 3rd or second to last place, but you can try, and you'll be better for it than if you didn't. Dead last, and you've still made steps in the right direction. You will likely be in better shape than anyone who isn't training for something like that.
Get my drift?

The other half is kindness. Be a decent human being.
I will break down attitude and kindness but kindness can encompass both. Kindness is about selflessly giving. For me it's my time. "I can't give you a bag of money, but I can give you my t me."
When giving someone time, they typically know that time is valuable, and it can get awkward, but spending 10 minutes sweeping the floor alongside somebody allows you to work at eye level.

A lot of leadership books and gurus say to be careful with your time, but I have found that when time is more valuable, it always comes back in a more meaningful way. So, Mr. Guru, I'm sorry, but I'm giving my time as Oprah gives away cars. "And you get some time, you get some time, look under your seat…. More time!"

I'm not sugarcoating anything here. It's what I believe are the building blocks of leadership. You need to come up with your style and brand; It will define who you are and how you operate as a leader, mentor, friend, sibling, spouse or parent.

The next part is optimizing your people. Their output at 100%, may only be your 80%, and that's ok. How can we optimize our people to operate at 110%? We do this through leadership, which is kindness, effective communication and attitude.

The last part of all of this is Realistic Expectations. If you have the kindness part, then you shouldn't struggle with the expectations part, but I think it needs to be said. Set expectations, and when they are met, reward people. I think there is a word for this. Ah yes, Integrity. Seems easy enough, right? Then why do so many people struggle with it?

Again, this is supposed to be a guide. It's what has worked really well for me, and I'm simply sharing it. I don't think you need to wake up at 3 am every day. Hu rah style. I don't think you need to have a strict diet or go to the gym. I think that you develop traits as you grow in your journey, and they tend to be healthy ones. I like having a clear mind so I can help solve problems, so it prevents me from going on mid-week benders with the boys at the bar. I like to be able to keep up with all of my guys physically, so I hit the gym. I wake up early to get my emails done and out of the way so I can be present at work and for my team.I believe these are steps towards leadership. Thinking about others before yourself.

I understand that there are people that need structure. So, having a busy wake-up schedule might be key for you, but it's one of those things that drive me mad when reading these leadership books. It feels like a gimmick. It should happen naturally because you need to succeed to help others succeed.Think of it as learning the guitar. You can memorize scales and finger positions, and it's mundane, and it works. However, when you understand music theory and why your scales seem to lock up with a chord that's matched to a key. It all makes sense, and naturally, your skill level skyrockets.

Leadership is the same way. If you want to get 80% out of your team and you're happy with that, then follow a program. If you want to get 120% out of your team, then learn to grow.

I'm just here trying to cultivate you; you are my flower. Let this guide be a little bit of fertilizer; now go, grow.

Ok, lastly, before we start. I am just a normal dude who has finally decided to put some thoughts on paper. I am nothing special. I hold no special titles before my name or college degrees. In fact, I'm a college dropout.
I have, however, been successful in my career managing people.

For the record, I am Forklift certified.

EFFECTIVE COMMUNICATION

What is effective communication?

Communicating a language that the person you are trying to convey can understand the easiest. Seems basic. Right?

How many times have you seen an English-speaking person try to talk to someone who doesn't really know English? They talk louder and slower. Which then becomes yelling really slow…. "CAN YOOOUUUU UNNNDDEERRSTTTANDD MEEE NNNOOOOOWW?" Who in the world thinks that helps anything? Apply that to the job, an interaction at the grocery store, or even a relationship. I'm not talking about just in their native language. I'm talking about the nuances of communication.

What's the golden rule? Treat others the way they want to be treated.

Speak to others the way they want to be spoken to in the clearest, most effective way possible.

That about sums it up.

(Feel free to skip to the next chapter. The rest is not going to be on the test.)

You're still with me.

Let's dive a little deeper.

How does this make me a better leader? It doesn't.

Sorry, Charlie. I wish it were that easy.

It does get your point across. It eliminates the third grade, he said she said. Our language gives us so many ways to convey a message. It allows you to be specific. If done correctly, allows confidence that you are setting your people up for success.

English is not my Dad's first language. Growing up, Dad would say something that made sense to him, but we would have to interpret what he was saying. Of course, if I did exactly what he said, we would get into trouble because "you knew what I meant". I see this a lot where there is a misuse of a term, or you should "know what I mean". Then, in a passive-aggressive attempt, everyone would get hung up on semantics.

Effective communication should try to both interpret to the best of your ability and ask questions if there is direction unclear.

Effective communication should also try to describe what's being told to the best of your ability and ask follow-up questions to ensure clarity.

Let's deep dive into ways you can effectively communicate.
Let's start with the literal sense of the term.

Document Everything

An easy way to be a very effective communicator is simply keeping all communication in a written format. The problem here is that you start to look like that guy. The guy or gal that nobody likes because he or she writes everything down. It solves the problem but doesn't get you much closer to being an effective leader.

This is a difference between leadership and just being a really good note-taker. I've used this as a first step when I have someone who is having a hard time communicating. I tel l them to document everything.

I have a pretty good memory when it comes to this stuff, but I still write down everything every evening before bed in my notes app on my phone. Nothing crazy, but it does help me to remember who I've talked to and why. I do this specifically so that when I wake up, I can start planning my day. Not to hold a conversation against someone or prove myself right. That's not helpful. I mean, I know I'm right… right (my wife slowly shaking her head no)?

I notice that when used as a first step, sometimes the person I've recommended this to walks around with a black book and a smug look. As they are having a conversation, they're writing down notes like a detective in a bad noir-style film. "Can you repeat what you just said? I want to make sure I get it down just right so I can use it against you later and make you look bad." I get that you now have a log of what was said, and you look like you're smarter than everyone else. We are talking about leadership here.
Use (clap) **your** (clap) **head** (clap) **detective** (clap) **dumb**.

This technique can help you, and it can hurt you. If you have integrity and do what you say you are going to do, then writing things down will help validate honesty. If you're a slimeball, then keeping things in email or text format will hurt you. Alright, so write it down but don't be a piece of poop. I think we've flushed this topic out.
(Really bad joke, I'm sorry, I can't help it.)

Less Talking and More Listening

Some people call it active listening. The art of listening and then being a part of the conversation. Nodding your head. Gasping when appropriate. Active listening means dropping the ego. To be an effective leader means not making everything about you. Make it about everyone else. Everybody wants to be heard. Just listening can allow someone to work through their problem, solve it, and then, in the end, thank you for being the guy or gal who fixed it. Think of a boss or manager that you've had, the second you start talking, interrupt and have to one-up you. Or they already have the answer.

Often, an employee, friend or significant other doesn't want the problem solved; they just want you to listen and then share their emotions with them at that moment.

Think about that for a second.
Read it again.

The cherry on top of that is reacting with them. "My dog died today." (This is tragic, but I needed it to get the point across.) Nothing needs to be solved here, so it's obvious they want you to listen. The cherry on this one is showing some empathy. More specifically, drop your head, perhaps you place your hand on their shoulder. That kind of stuff.

Another one that comes to mind is when someore is mad; they want you to be mad with them. This is tricky and a fine line to walk. Sometimes, it helps just to stay stoic and give them some room to vent.I have a hard time in this department. I have been accused of not showing emotion. If this is you, a word of caution is that it's better to be a poker face than a phony.

Pro tip: It's an easy thing to ask, "Am I solving problems, or am I listening?" I do this at home with my wife.
Often, I'm just listening.

"Am I solving problems or am I listening?" is powerful and has a way of putting things in perspective.

An example is Todd is upset that he can't get along with Tammy. It's affecting his work output. So I make my rounds for the day and offer a few minutes of my time, and Todd starts to rant about Tammy and their work relationship. I ask, "Am I solving problems or listening?" Todd realizes he's being a spreader of strife and immediately solves his problem. He thanks you for the help, and you move on to ask him how his hockey game went over the weekend. See what you did there? Really, nothing, but you had the wherewithal to allow Todd to

work through his stuff. Todd is going to think that you solved his problems for the day, and you will be the hero in his eyes.
The alternative here is he really does need help, and you are able to identify a major problem. You determine the need to mediate a conversation with both of them to solve their issue.
Still coming out of the hero.

At one point, while working on the railroad. I was working in Essex, MT. I was a mechanic, and the equipment was out plowing snow, so we were on standby waiting for a breakdown. If your equipment was working and people were out plowing, then this was a good thing. Your day started when the equipment came back to the shop in the late afternoon/evening. This meant we didn't have much to do while waiting around, but we did have an internet connection, so I decided I wanted to become an active listener at the time; there was an online service that you could become certified for free that allows you to be on the receiving end of a help hotline but through messaging. Sort of a suicide prevention hotline but done via a web browser and typing. Once certified and practice interactions were done, I spent the next few weeks interacting with people who were struggling with life and learned very quickly how to listen and ask questions. The difference between a crisis and just someone needing to vent. The lesson here was I needed to offer kind words and a listening ear. It's like magic, and people open up. They will pour their hearts out. I heard all kinds of crazy things. It felt good to help someone, and there was an occasion I actually had to call in a wellness check. Maybe that one interaction saved a life; I will never know. Perhaps in another life, I will get the opportunity to be a counselor. The point here is listening.

Listening is a skill. It's very hard when a topic comes up in conversation that really applies to you, and you want to shout it out at the top of your lungs so everyone can hear how awesome you are. Well, the truth of the matter is that nobody really cares. Sorry.
The person talking is more excited to talk about themselves. So plug it up. This is a salesman tactic. Build
rapport, ask questions, share one but only one personal experience and then let the customer speak. Ask more questions. You're building

them up and making them feel good for the big purchase. They don't care about your stories. It's their special day. Not yours.

Just Less Talking

If you're shy, to begin with, then skip this part. This is for the people who overcomplicate things by talking too much.

The best example of this is back in the railroad days when we would talk over the radio. The goal is to speak the most information you can give in the shortest amount of words possible effectively. If I'm giving you a task, then I need to be clear in my direction, confident in my delivery, and then set a goal or expectation.

You may think that reiterating it in different ways over and over so you may be better understood helps, but you are just mudding up the waters, pal.

Straight and to the point. Ask questions to confirm that the direction is clear and reiterate if necessary. The same still applies when listening. See, not so hard.

I've been told that I like to build clocks instead of telling the time. Sometimes, it's necessary to build a clock for context; other times, it is necessary to tell the time.

The next part of this is asking yourself if you are being a spreader of strife. I see this in people who like to talk to hear their voices. It's easy for a leader to overshare something that can be taken out of context. Next thing you know, you have people thinking they are all being fired, and you've just thrown a bucket of stress into the workplace. Remember, you're a leader so that people will listen to you. "With great power comes great responsibility, Peter."

Perhaps you're not a leader yet, but you're in a position of authority. You can spread strife easier, so take a chill, Bill.

"Boy, nobody realized the stress I have to deal with. I am dealing with this and that and this, and I have to babysit all of you." You have just reduced the confidence of whoever you just told that to by a point or two. I'm not saying fake it, but you need to be the person you're people can lean on.

Wait. You know what, let's make this one easy and keep your whining to yourself. Less talking.

Identify Commonalities

To be able to communicate means breaking the ice. You need to connect first. Then, get down to business. A really good way to connect to someone is to find something you know a little bit about. For example when I meet someone for the first time, I am like Robocop scanning everything they are wearing, what vehicle they drive, how they speak. All of it. I am Sherlock Holmes'ing my way into a conversation that I can own.

An example of this is when I meet John for the first time and notice he is wearing a hat with an airplane on it. I use a little deduction to see that it's a Cessna 150. I happen to know one thing about flying, so I start the conversation with. "You fly planes?" he responds with," Not yet, but I'm taking lessons." Boom, I got him. Hook, line and sinker. "Oh, awesome; I used to mow an airstrip for my neighbors as a kid, and in exchange, he would take me flying in his little Cessna 150 every Friday. (see what I did there?)
I also have been through ground school but never finished. What is your favorite part about flying? I'm sure it's changed a lot since I did it."

I have started a meaningful conversation, and now I store that in the old memory bank; I've built rapport, have something to follow up with next time, and I've broken the ice. Notice, it wasn't all about me. I needed to give some personal information, but like a good salesman, I changed the conversation back to him and his favorite part of flying. It doesn't have to be about flying or even their hat. It can be anything you can make a connection with. You can do it with anything. Maybe it's their accent, shoes, or sunglasses. Who knows, that's part of the fun.

Commonalities and rapport are essential. It's what makes you seem human. Think of a person who is obsessed with one thing. Think about how they will shift the conversation to be on the topic of their thing. This is because they are comfortable in that space. They are comfortable, so they open up. The problem is that if it's not your thing, then you distance yourself. See, this is a subtle game of tug of war. The key here is to be comfortable being uncomfortable. You only need to know a couple of key points in a topic to have a conversation about it. If the interaction starts getting too deep, then admit that you don't know a lot about it.

Imagine if my fake conversation with John had shifted where he was asking me technical questions about a Cessna. It's an easy thing to deflect. "Ha, you know it was a long time ago, and heaven forbid you hand me over the controls when you get your license because I've watched Top Gun too many times." A little joke counter move, and you still have this as a talking point the next time you see him and can still follow up with him on how his lessons are going. All we needed was the ability to start a conversation and something that could connect us in the future.

When I was on the safety team, we would travel around and spend a lot of time in airports and hotels for seminars. My safety partner and I had the idea to challenge the other person to grab a bit of information that might seem tough in a 5-minute interaction. I would get challenged to talk to an old man standing opposite me. The goal would be to find out if he has kids, how many, and what their names are. Extra points if I could get their ages. So you get creative and have to find a commonality quickly and then figure out how you were going to smoothly transition into getting this information out of him. We played it enough that we were pros. What we didn't realize at the time, what seemed like an interesting way to pass the time, was actually setting ourselves up for leadership. Being able to make someone comfortable with us in a short period and then build rapport for our next interaction.

We would often take this another step. You see, I was a pro at breaking the ice and warming them up. He was a pro at being a salesman. We'd be in an electronic store. Casually see someone looking at the newest tech, and that was our target. I would take the lead at breaking the ice, and then he would swoop in and create a case as to why they needed this tech in their life. By the time we were done they'd have maxed out a credit card and were the proud new owners of a laptop or iPad that they never knew they needed. Actually, they most likely would never even use it.

I challenge you to try this on. Find a commonality with a stranger and spark up a conversation. It's easy and fun. Get good at it, and who knows who you'll meet.

ATTITUDE

Not anyone else's attitude. This is about you, babe.
I had a job interview one time where I was so underqualified it hurt.
I'm pretty sure they just needed someone else to interview, so the guy
that was getting the job had someone that could lose. That loser, me. I
was already a little irritated that I was told to interview against my will.
Although, I thought it would be funny if somehow I managed to get it. I
knew that wasn't going to happen, but it was a great opportunity to
practice my interview skills. Once I saw the job description, I realized
that I had zero experience, like a negative amount of experience. I
didn't meet any of the minimum requirements. It would be the
equivalent of my great-grandmother applying for a coding job in
Silicon Valley for Chat GPT4. The kicker is my great-grandmother isn't
even alive. May she rest in peace. So, I like the Wylie Coyote I am. I
start scheming up a plan. The plan is to focus on the only skill I have
that I could apply, and that's a good attitude.

 I opened with something like, "I have zero skills that pertain to this
job; I have zero knowledge or formal training. I have no experience. I
actually don't really even want the job; however I have a really good
attitude. (It was here I smiled and paused for an awkwardly long
period) If I end up getting the job and am asked to scrub the toilets,
you can bet on me doing it with a smile on my face. I have an
appreciation for life. I have an appreciation for employment and
supporting my family. I am not beneath any task or any of my peers. I
am willing to learn and will put my best foot forward every day. I put
others before myself. I am honest. I have no ego. I understand the
value of this position and what it can do for my career. My goal is to
continue my way up the company ladder, so if given the opportunity, I
will do my best with the goal in mind that my actions speak louder
than words. You can count on me to be at least 15 minutes early to
work and stay as long as necessary to get the job done."
It was a little something like that. The panel was in shock. I was
beaming a smile from ear to ear. I had just hit them with a left hook,
and they never saw it coming.

I was told it was the best interview ever given. I still didn't get the job, but it became a whole thing, and it was recorded and used later on for training.

What I said is true. I'm a glass-half-full guy with an appreciation for waking up in the morning. I'm not saying I don't have my bad days, but I know that if I flip that switch that says, "I'm appreciative," That shows. People take notice. It's the smile on your face. Let's talk about leadership here. Leaders motivate. Having the right attitude is motivating and contagious.

I challenge you to try that on for a day. Find a reason to give a compliment and then follow up with a fist bump or high five. It will go a long way. The coolest part about this is its reciprocation.
Be your hype, man, then hype up others. It's amazing how quickly the people you engage with will become the first to give you a fist bump or hype you up for the day. We all need a little joy, and that's a really low-hanging fruit way to get it.

No Task Is Below Me

This is hard. I've seen this a million times. Give someone a fancy title, and all of a sudden, they want to do a whole lot of sitting around and refuse to do any labor. Sorry pal. Leadership means seeing your people at eye level.

When I was in the safety program, I would travel around and meet with other fellow mechanics. It's no secret that safety people are hated. I was no exception. So, how do I shift this paradigm? Well, for starters, I would pack my tools on the plane, and instead of just being the bad guy, I would show up as a helping hand. "What can I do that would make your life easier? You have me for a day." Of course, I got the shit jobs, but I was excited and motivated and did my best. I was looking at what tools they had and did a truck inspection and would educate not regulate. "This strap is no longer good to use. It is no longer good to use because of the grease and the tear here. I understand you need it to do your job, so I am ordering you a new one right now. What's a good address I can get the three new ones I just ordered sent?" It didn't take long for my presence to be a welcoming one. I like to think that I created a movement, but as you can guess, there aren't a lot of people willing to do extra work if they didn't have to. This was a way to connect. I didn't reed to identify a commonality when the commonality was the job or task at hand.

Pretend that you have to dig a hole. Now, you can rule with an iron fist. It's effective, and it works, but you're not going to get 100% out of your people. They are going to show up for a paycheck and do the bare minimum. That's fine if that's how you operate. It does the job. I find that in areas where the labor pool is really large, this is the predominant philosophy. "Do what I say when you're on my time because there are a hundred other pecple who would love this job". You can make your people dig your hole for you with this mentality. Don't expect it to be quick. Don't expect it to be perfect. "I'm only here for a paycheck, right?"

Let's not be like that if we are trying to optimize our people. (which you will read about in a bit) Now, say you have ten people to dig the hole. You're a busy guy whose time is valuable. The hole will take each person 30 minutes to dig. You jump in there and dig shoulder to shoulder at your 100% and are happy to be there for just 5 minutes out of their 30; you see where I'm going with this? Five minutes is no sweat off your back. I mean, it will be a total of 50 minutes, but you know what? We are here to motivate.

This is leadership.

Help Me Help You Help Me Help You Win

Allowing me to help you win helps me win. Why wouldn't we all want to win? It boggles my mind when I see this idea of "I want to win, and I want it to all be me and my win and nobody else." These people seem like little kids. They are everywhere. I'm sorry you didn't get to be team captain at recess or something. It seems desperate.

During my career, for a period when I taught rules, I traveled six days a week all over the country. It was a salary job and there was no life other than railroad. Now, a new policy had just been implemented that if an employee didn't pass the annual rules test, then they would be taken out of service and forced to go to a week-long class with the new hires to be given another opportunity to pass it. If they didn't get it that time, then they got kicked to the curb. (I'm not sure that actually happened, but the threat was there.)

You can imagine how some of the old heads responded to this news. There was a lot of hatred for the rules teachers. Now, some major changes were the catalyst for the drastic measures. It was all new and complicated. Even some of the rules teachers didn't have a solid grasp on the new stuff.

My performance was based on my class's test scores. It paid literally to have the classes I taught do well on the test. Doing well on the test paid literally to the people who took it because it kept them employed. Hmmm, I went to the drawing board. How can I ensure my guys win so I can win and get that bonus?

My idea was to do a study group the night before. Seemed like common sense to me. I was on the road, and I had to eat anyway. I would email the class I was to teach the next day where I was planning on having dinner and the time. Typically, it was in some small town, so the only place to eat was the local watering hole. They were welcome to meet me for dinner or a beer, and then we would go over the next day's material. Then, when I taught the class, those who were in the study group would help others learn. It became so popular that I would have 20-plus people meet me to study. It became a fun thing, and my failure rate was 0%.

The moral here is I need my people to win so I can win. Sounds selfish. It's not. There is a symbiotic relationship in a team. If it's balanced right, everyone comes out a winner. Allow your people to win. Set them up for success. I've said it before but drop your ego.

In the end, I needed good test scores; they needed to pass. It forced me to care about their success, and it forced them to take advantage of the additional help I was offering. It forced me to care about them as colleagues and what would evolve into my friends. Who doesn't want their friends to win?

Ever have a supervisor who claims they care about their people? Most people chalk that up to bullshit. They care about their injury report reading zero. They care about what is going to get them a bonus at the end of the year. What I've since realized is that if there is that symbiotic relationship and people who really do care, eventually, it isn't always about padding the wallet; it is about caring.

I went to a clinic in Virginia where I listened to Dr.Scott Gellar, the inventor of "Actively caring for people," and he said, "What if we all just care about each other? Like everyone was our best friend or our brother or sister, son, daughter?"

That symbiotic relationship I'm talking about reciprocates.
When we all want the win, if we all care for each other, then it doesn't become about padding the wallet or the zero injury report. It humanizes us. Once that clicked, I thought back to the supervisors who actually did care, and that is leadership, my friend.

There's No I... Ever

Allowing your team to win means giving them credit when they do. Remember that hole we are digging even though you spent 5 minutes with all ten people, which equals 50 minutes, where everyone else spent 30 minutes each. So technically, you spent more time digging than any one person, but that doesn't mean you get to claim any of the credit. Your team dug the hole. They, we. As a leader, these are your pronouns. You are your team.

Here's one to try on. I challenge you to try taking out the words I and me from your vocabulary for the week. Even if someone worked on the project for a short period, they get the credit for it. Especially when talking to a higher-up.

It's a knee-jerk to claim ownership of a project or show off what you accomplished. Trust me, you will be seen as a leader and go further if you take zero credit and give it all to your people. I've been on factory tours where the manager takes credit for everything in the factory. He gives zero notice to anyone who's working. It can still be impressive, but it didn't do anything for his rapport with his people. The people he toured saw right through him, and he lost some credibility.
Instead, stopping at each section and allowing that employee to explain briefly what they are working on, then saying something like, "Without Gina, we wouldn't be able to move forward," empowers the employee and builds trust.
That's leadership.

There was an older railroad mechanic who was probably the smartest there was. He has since retired and now works on race cars and complains about politics.

You could describe what was going on, making clicking sounds, and he could give a proper diagnosis right there. He would say, "If man can build it, then man can fix it," and let me tell you, he would. What's interesting about this story is he never took credit for anything. If you were just in the area, he gave you credit for the repair or diagnosis. As an outsider looking in, I could tell you it made him an even better mechanic. You felt like he was humble, and it built trust. It also made more people question who this guy was, and he became a living legend. You would think that since he's giving away all the credit, he would live in the shadows, but the opposite is true.
Take note here.

It can be tough to give away credit for something you've put blood, sweat and tears into, but it doesn't go unnoticed. You will be better for it.

I challenge you to find something you can give away credit for and see how it makes you feel. See how it makes others feel.

** I initially wrote this section without the use of words with the letter "I" since there is no "I" in the team. You're welcome. I threw that draft straight into the garbage. **

Change Your Paradigm

If you are not a glass-half-full type of person, then change that. Today. Right now. Not sure I have any secret sauce here for you, but you need to be an optimistic person. Have you ever seen a leader that walks around like Eeyore all day? No, you haven't. Your team can. Not you. You need to find optimism in everything. Keep up that morale for the team. Even in their failures or your own. This is really important. I wish I had a magic pill that could make everyone optimistic, but I know that we are not all wired that way. Find some stress relief, take up a hobby, and see a therapist. Whatever you need to do to get on the positive side of all of it, do it.

I told you I wasn't going to sugarcoat this.
You'll find that if you can pull it off, then the rare times you are stressed or are down, if you have led your team the right way, they will boost you back up. They will catch you when you fall, and that's a cool feeling. You have to set the bar, and that starts with you. One bad apple can ruin the bunch. One negative person can take down the whole team. You're a leader; don't ruin the apples, Johnny.

Now, I have seen grumpy, pessimistic leaders. I'm not saying they aren't out there. I can't see a world where you would want to be one. If you want to be a grump and nicknamed Oscar the Grouch behind your back that is ok. I don't think that you are going to get the full potential out of your team. I've seen it plenty. You have some of the best leaders who are tough, rough and full of negativity. Maybe that's the culture of the line of work that you are in.

The difference is that if I think back on any of those leaders who were true leaders but ruled with an iron fist, they were always the smartest people in the room. They always had an answer and were confident. They were likely the first to arrive in the morning. They probably were the ones actually doing the work. They, even if you didn't realize it, were teaching. If this works for you and you're not interested in growth or optimization, then you may stop reading here.

In the evolution of growth, I think that happiness has a place in leadership. I think that full potential comes when morale or happiness is high for both parties.

I would compare this to praising kids. I would bet that a lot of you who are reading this were raised in a "you could always do better" home. "If you're not first, you're last."
"Should have practiced harder, and the team could have won."
"You should have got an A on that test. You must not have studied hard enough."

A lot of you probably think, "Look at me; I turned out fine. Kids these days are too soft." Well, Bud, that's not the world we live in. The world we live in promotes praise and kindness.

In 1998, Arcaro Dwek did a study that helped form the culture we are leaning towards today. If you are not familiar with it, she studied the effects of praise regardless of test scores in kids. She and her colleagues found that those who were given praise, even if the kids did poorly on the test, their scores started to go up. This is actually called Non-Contingent reinforcement. They were given a mindset to overcome challenges and not give up. The kids that were put down and shamed gave up easily, and test scores plummeted. They became too fearful to try. They were living in shame.

Think about that next time your team doesn't quite meet the goal. Try to experiment and see how they respond to all positive feedback. See how the energy feels after that conversation or meeting. Maybe the next time they fly by the goal and all because of a small paradigm shift. Maybe next time, they will work harder to adapt and overcome because they feel empowered.

That is leadership.

OPTIMIZING YOUR PEOPLE

We all would love to have a team of rock stars. Just super high IQ individuals who work well with others and who can think for themselves. If that was the case, then why wouldn't they start their own company? The fact of the matter is you get what you get. You might be stuck with a jack wagon for an employee, peer or even a supervisor. You can optimize that person to be the best they can be. Optimizing your people is a conversation I love to have. Is it possible to optimize your people to meet your expectations? Are you setting expectations? Are they realistic, and are you giving them the tools they need to succeed?

When I mention optimizing a supervisor or boss, people usually cock their heads to one side and give me a blank stare. You can optimize them, too. As an employee who is a leader, you can give your boss the tools they need to succeed. Make their lives easier, and just like everything else, it reciprocates. Don't be a brown noser. Nobody likes that. Be on point. Have answers. Work hard. Catch the pieces that fall through the cracks. Where there is a void. Fill it.

I have a dog that will do anything my wife says. He only does what I say about half the time when nobody else is around. It's because my wife has optimized him for success with her. She has put in the work and training. I'm sure if I put in the same amount of work, I could see those results as well. I'm totally not comparing people to training dogs, but I am comparing the amount of work that goes into a good relationship. A little elbow grease goes a long way. She has shown good leadership and has a well-trained well behaved dog.

You know, an argument could be made that my dog has optimized my wife to work for him because he knows if he does all the tricks and is really good, he gets a carrot as a reward. He is a good employee that is on point and makes his supervisor look good. It's a symbiotic relationship, and they both come out happy and fulfilled, and that's all that matters.

Expectations

As much as we would like to think that a person can and should figure it out, it never works that way. Humans need expectations. Let's use our hole-digging scenario.

If I say, dig a hole. (not effective communication here). Let's say I have a background in excavation, and the backhoe is sitting around the corner. I assume you would grab the backhoe and start digging. I need a big hole. You don't know that, though. The backhoe doesn't even cross your mind. You go for a shovel. Not my expectation and you can see how this conversation is going to go.
I can't get upset because I didn't set expectations.

Another example is something that I like to share with newly married couples. If you were raised in a home where your mom did the cooking and cleaning and finances, and your partner was not. There is going to be an expectation there that may never be spoken about, but there will be a whole lot of animosity.

Let's apply this to leadership now. During my effective communication I set expectations. It allows for constructive conversations to take place that help with growth. Making sure that we both have the same thing in mind is healthy. "I need the hole dug; I hope we can get two dump truck loads out by the end of the day. There is a backhoe around the corner that you're free to use to make the job easier. If you haven't operated one, this would be a great opportunity for some training."

Everybody needs goals. Setting expectations and then when it is met, rewarding that behavior is really effective. Leadership means setting expectations that set your people up for success. Identifying their weaknesses and using all of your resources to build them from weaknesses to strengths.

Expectations are something that even if you think you have the perfect job description or have lined out the perfect amount of communication, can be tricky. The issue with expectations is you create a box that you now need to operate in. If I tell you I need two dump truck loads of dirt dug out and hauled at the end of the day, you have just applied a limit or glass ceiling on our overall potential. Maybe I will knock that out by noon, but if that's all that's been asked of me, then I'm going to work slowly to get the task done and not go above and beyond. Sound familiar?

Perhaps instead you ask how much dirt your operator thinks they can move by the end of the day, and then you help to motivate them to push a little bit beyond their limits. This is rewarding for both parties and is what leadership looks like.

The Moving Goalpost

Where expectations can be set that can be met with a hard win are great. More often than not, we have a star employee, friends or partners who, when the expectation is met, add more to their plate. We take advantage without knowing it. This moves the goalpost and becomes really frustrating. "Well, since you dug that hole so easily and so far ahead of schedule, let's try to dig one more by the end of the day". I mean, we have to keep our people busy if they are being paid, right? This is demotivating and trains your people to work slowly.

I understand that sometimes it's not affordable to send an employee home with pay because they got ahead, but here is where we get to think outside the box. "Well, since you dug that hole so far ahead of schedule if you guys push for a second hole in a day, I will BBQ and provide lunch to everyone to show my appreciation." This shows your willingness to put in your time to feed your people as a reward at little cost. It's an example, but you get the point.

It's also something we do in our everyday lives and relationships. When things are going really great, we tend to find things to bitch about. Everything is done, and all my expectations are met. My honey-do list is finished. This should be a sigh of relief, yet somehow, we are our own worst enemies. We then focus on the tree in the backyard that's too tall all of a sudden. You are moving the goalpost on yourself. You need to enjoy the wins. Allow your team, partner, friends and family to enjoy the wins.

Often, if I feel like I'm stressed and have a lot on my plate, then I want everyone to have a lot on their plate. I'm drowning, so I need everyone to be in misery with me. Sorry, Charlie. Lack of planning on your part does not constitute an emergency on my part. I have my work done. Your stress doesn't belong to anyone else. If you let it bleed over, then often you will find a reason to move the goalpost to make others busy. That's not fair, and it creates contention.

Tools for Success

Optimization means efficiency. Efficiency can be achieved through automation, tools, training and creature comforts. Setting people up for success means giving them what they need. When I say that, I mean what they think they need. I think this term gets thrown around a lot and gets overlooked. I have an employee who doesn't need a photo of his dog on his desk to do his job, but he did need a photo of his dog on his desk to be in the right mindset. To be in the right mindset to perform at 100%. It may seem silly, but it's the little things that make a difference.

Remember the golden rule.

Don't give someone what <u>you</u> think they need to succeed; give them what <u>they</u> think they need to succeed.

Of course, within reason. Don't be a fool and fall for the old. "We really need a popcorn machine in the depot to do our jobs and boost morale." I pulled that off one time. It was amazing, and we had popcorn at the end of every day, but I think we would have been just fine without it.

As you are reading through this, everything I am trying to give you is a tool. They are tools that helped me succeed. Pass these tools along so others can succeed. Of course, giving them a copy of this book helps me succeed. The tools for success are a culmination of all of the tips and tricks of the trade you have gathered along the way, plus the things that humanize and allow us to have some ownership.

I can't imagine that someone who works day in and day out in a cubicle with nothing from home on their desk or anything to look forward to except that the next smoke break is giving their 100%. It sounds like a robotic position that needs a body to fill it.
We could go down a really deep rabbit hole here talking about remote work and efficiency and humanizing roles, but this is supposed to be a field guide.

Tools and training are easy. It's the other things. This is leadership. Figure out what makes someone happy and implement that thing.

A study was done in the 70s by Robert K. Greenleaf, who coined the term Servant Leadership. The idea here is that prioritizing the needs of your team comes first. He has a whole list of really amazing leadership guidelines, which I encourage you to read about, but one that really applies here is:
Awareness, understanding the needs of yourself but also understanding the needs of your people and the dynamics of the environment in which they operate.

"Understand the dynamics of the environment in which they operate."

Spend time learning to understand this part, and you've just started to create a family dynamic.

Thanks Mr.Greenleaf.

We should talk about tools and training for a second. It's important. Tools and training.

Kindness

Kindness goes a long way to optimizing a person. This could deserve a whole chapter, but I think you get it, or you don t. Be kind. Pretty simple.

Apply kindness to everything. As a leader, you can lead and get things done and be firm, but you can also be kind.
Imagine if you needed to dig that hole we've been talking about on a weekend. How many friends could you call and dig that hole with you for free? How many employees could you call that would do that for you? If you have shown enough kindness, then it wouldn't even be a conversation. It's a good thought experiment to see just how kind you are.

I was leaving work to go home for the day after a long week and noticed an employee washing his vehicle with the company pressure washer. An act of the type of kindness 'm talking about is immediately grabbing a sponge and helping him clean his rig. Remember, I can't give out bags of money, but I can give away my time. He was appreciative, and we were able to talk about work. It allowed me to get a pulse as to what was happening with the boots-on-the-ground employees. For that short amount of time, he was my boss. I was just there to assist.

Like any good sports movie where the coach needs to motivate the team, there's always this moment where he becomes one of the guys. He is on their level and gains their respect.

An argument could be made that you've compromised your role in authority. I say, who cares? It doesn't sound like you were confident in that role or did it well to begin with. Ouch, burn. It's a hard pill to swallow.

It's worth saying that kindness should always be selfless. If you are doing it to bank a favor for yourself later, then don't bother. It will come back around. Just be patient.

LEADERS BECOME SOMEONE'S MENTOR

Have a Person

Having a person refers to the Grey's Anatomy episode, where they all have people they can lean on. Remember that one? Ok, well, it's like having a really good friend who will listen when it is important but will also call you out when you have a booger hanging out your nose. That's exactly what I'm talking about here. As leaders, we need that one person we can lean on. The boots on the ground, guy. Not a spy, a mole, or a rat. Just a person. The one you trust to catch things that fall through the cracks.

When trying to help make a supervisor successful as a leader, I have him or her identify the one person who would make their lives easier if they had them in their pocket. Then, I make it their goal to form a relationship with that person. Daily check-ins or a quick morning briefing. Having someone who truly wants you to win and perhaps is a leader in their way will help set you up for success and vice versa. Ideally, you should have that person that you call on your drive home from work who fills you in on their successes and their failures. You plan for the next day and set yourself up for success.

It's important to have someone you can lean on, and then you are there for someone else to lean on. This is a natural progression in the journey of leadership. Imagine a world where you don't even have to tell your team to do anything. It just gets done. You have that person who takes charge and makes your life easy because you've set them all up for success.

<u>You know you might be that person for someone else.</u>
Think about that one.

Gate Keeping

Mentorship and leadership are about wanting your peers to grow faster than you do. Don't gatekeep. If you have a skill or piece of knowledge, for crying out loud. Share it Remember, we want our team to win to help us win. Why do it?

It's our insecurities that make us withhold information. Stop it. Confidence is a sign of a great leader. When you start sharing everything you know, you'll get a reputation as a teacher. Teacher = leader = mentor…. See the evolution here, you wise owl.
We gate keep for our gain. It's not a good look.
It's a passive-aggressive behavior that can be really tough to overcome. If you have pissed me off and I have a piece of information that will make life easier for you, you can bet I'm not coughing it up to help you. Not cool.

The other thing that has become more normal is the idea that I'm not doing anything without compensation. This may be old school, but I believe you are obligated to your company to do everything in your power to help the overall success. I understand that in the short term, it may seem unfair, but in the long run, you'll be noticed, and you will be the one who has a job during the layoff season, or you will be the one getting that promotion.

An example is being bilingual. You work at a restaurant, and a family comes in, speaking a language that you understand. You are a dishwasher, and it's not in your job description to translate. You are now faced with a choice. Do you demand additional compensation? Or do you step up and translate? The choice is yours, but it will be noticed and asking for a raise or promotion will be a whole lot easier than had you been difficult. The other side to this is that if you've built a business that sets everyone up for success and they want the overall win, then I bet your employee has no problem stepping up for you. It's that reciprocation I mentioned earlier.

Now, that is a literal sense of the term gatekeeping. It happens in far more subtle ways where that passive-aggressive thing you read earlier takes place. Maybe an email gets sent, and you forget to add a cc. Or perhaps you give some information but not all of the information necessary. Karate chop that behavior in half.

Isn't This Manipulation?

I often find myself pondering the fine line that separates effective leadership or mentorship from outright manipulation. This thought struck me particularly hard during an exchange of 'identifying commonalities' and establishing rapport with a team member. It dawned on me that, in his eyes, I had become more than a boss – I was his best friend. Yet, to me, he remained an employee. He wanted to be buddies and was treating me unprofessionally. This realization brought an uncomfortable awareness of a boundary crossed. It's an easy trap to take advantage of that perception.

This person had never been shown kindness. So, to him, I was his best friend, and that's OK. Unprofessionalism is not.
At this point, I needed to establish some healthy work-life and personal life boundaries in order to move forward.

"You're a great team member, and I'm here to support you, but we have to remember I'm still your boss." I made sure he knew this didn't change anything about the help and advice I'd keep giving him at work.

What else I realized is that it's not manipulation if there is a balance on both sides of the exchange. What I mean by that is by making someone happy and optimizing my employee he then is willing to go above and beyond. There is mutual respect, and equilibrium of work exchanged. I am providing my time and setting my team up for success, and they are willing to give me that little bit extra.

There is a fine line here, though. Not being genuine can easily turn what you think is equilibrium into what they perceive as manipulation. That's a bad look, and the quickest way for your team to form a mutiny is to tie your feet together and bounce you off the plank into Davy Jones's locker.

Manipulation, by definition, is to change by unfair means. What is fair? It's having integrity.

This is another golden rule example. If what you are doing is not being interpreted as fair, then either some expectations were not established, communication was not done effectively, or it's not fair.

"It's not fair that I have to work the weekend." It may not be, however, if you're being compensated at a rate of time and a half, then all of a sudden, we have created equilibrium. Sometimes, to lead effectively, we need to put those things into perspective.

There is a local job that is paying its technician $200k a year. It's a gross overpayment of the kind of work this individual will be doing. I'm paying my technician $85k a year, which is at the top end of the pay scale in our area. I also provide 401k and health insurance. My guy jumps ship and quickly realizes that the $200k a year doesn't include the two helpers he needs to hire at $50k each. The materials he will use to complete the job. He gets no benefits, and the work environment sucks.
Had I put that into perspective, and he understood, we could have quickly ended that perception of unfairness or manipulation.

Leadership is about adding context and perspective.

Healthy Boundaries

Establishing healthy boundaries has a lot of meaning, so let's break it down. First things first, since you are a team leader, boss, and supervisor, your time is valuable. Even if you're not one of those things, you should act like your time is valuable. Don't get taken advantage of. Be considered when giving away your time. Remember, I can't give you a bag of cash, but I can give you my time. That time may only be 5 minutes, but I'm here for it.

Early in my career, I suffered from always saying yes to everyone and doing everything for free. I would be the guy that you could call at 2 am, and I would help you move. It got in the way of my marriage and became a problem. I've always seen my time as free, so it was never a big deal to me. Once I realized that I needed to be careful about my time, things changed. I started getting asked to help with only important things. I re-established myself. I quit apologizing for not being available. Now, when I get asked for my time, it's usually things that are challenging and fun.

The next part of this is to be careful getting too close. It's ok if that's your plan, but remember that when someone sees you as a friend or a bro, then it becomes ok for them to get special treatment or get away with things that may not actually be cool. The boundary here is maybe you skip out on going with the team getting plastered on Wednesday night at the bar. You can still lead effectively and not be everyone's buddy-buddy but still be everyone's buddy.
Get what I mean?

The last part of that is now that you're becoming a leader. You need to set healthy work boundaries for yourself. We will talk about stress later, but it is possible to lead so effectively that you can go home and turn your phone off for the evening. Establish these boundaries early on. I understand that the real world may mean you are on call or putting in some crazy long days, but learn to delegate and be your own best advocate. "My time is valuable; my family comes first." You will gain respect there. That's confidence. You will get walked on if you let people walk on you. It's just the way that it is.

THE JOURNEY

Personal Growth

There is a natural progression of personal growth. Notice that I am not saying you need to stay out of the bar, become an athlete, or do any of those things to be a leader. It's a natural progression. The Ah-hah moment will hit you when you want your team to win. In order to get that win, you start drinking more water because you suffer from chronic headaches that don't help with being on point. Or perhaps you need more energy in the day, and you realize that working out allows you to perform better physically. These are a natural progression. It's all part of personal growth.

You'll start to connect the dots. If I wake up an hour earlier, I can get a few things done that cut some stress out in the evening. I didn't have to sacrifice anything, but I've managed to create efficiency in both my personal and work life. You start seeing a therapist and learn some of the lingo, and the next thing you know, you're using the same skills to help manage your people. See how this works.

Read something good for your personal relationship, perhaps you learn to adapt it to your professional relationships. Another progression for the win. Helping yourself helps you lead, and effectively leading creates wins for the team. It's a win-win for everyone.

There are a lot of people out there who tell you the habits of leaders or successful people. That's great! Run with it. Be sure to ask yourself why. What caused this person to change their lifestyle this way? The more you can look inward and understand, the better informed you are to implement it in a meaningful way.

The one that gets me is hearing that you need to wake up incredibly early. I see that all the time. I think that it's a byproduct of necessity. Sleep is important. If you can't get it at night, take naps. In my eyes,

the people who are claiming you need to sleep 4 hours a night to be effective are not efficient with their time. Or they nap a lot.
Think about honing in yourself so you can be super-efficient. Perhaps you can get your day down to 4 hours. That means more sleep for you and no crankiness.

I also see the "This is what I do in a day," and it's so unrealistic. Who has time to wake up and do yoga for an hour, then have a chef-made meal before an hour of tennis? Let's be realistic. Sometimes, we are lucky if we get a granola bar on the way out of the door.

Set small, realistic goals. Maybe you read for 10 minutes before starting your day. It's not much, but it's something. A start, and what I'm telling you is it is all a natural progression from there.

Team Growth

Part of leadership is promoting growth. That's where that whole mentorship thing comes in. If you're trying to grow, it's easy to share a book or knowledge with someone else.

Be wary, though; like a vegan or a cross-fitter, unless somebody cares…. Nobody cares.

An easy way to give someone a little boost is to tell them you've noticed their growth and want to help in any way that you can. Offer advice and allow them to lean on you. I know you're so excited to have read this book and tell everyone you meet about it. Easy cowboy. Use your new skill and build rapport first. Shoving leadership down anyone's throat isn't going to make them a better anything.

I often see people in leadership positions keep their employees from moving up or starting their own business, or pursuing a passion due to fear of losing them. Gatekeeping…. Again, this is all about leadership, and leadership is about selflessness. You should want the very best for your team. Be excited and help them grow. Unfortunately, we find that rock star of an employee, and they are such a key part of the team that we sometimes block their route. If you've created a business that will stand the test of time, then each position should be replaceable.

Furthermore, if you are a great leader, then most people will feel content and happy where they are. When promoting team growth, it's important that everyone feels like they make a difference in the outcome of the project, company and team.

Accountability

Leadership can be a lonely road. Surround yourself with others who are on the same journey you are. Hold yourself accountable. Hold your peers accountable. That whole "surround yourself with the people you want to aspire to" holds value. Surround yourself with true friends, and likely, those friends will be on this leadership journey with you.

I called three friends who are business owners to meet for breakfast and jokingly called it an accountability and leadership meeting. I had no intention of making it a thing. I had no agenda or topic of discussion. For our first breakfast, we spent the entire time deep-diving into our struggles and leadership techniques. It went so well that everyone wanted to do another one the following week. It taught me that we all want to be better leaders and that we all need someone to bounce things off of and a support group.

Again, this was just a natural progression of leadership. I suppose you could say that writing this book is just another natural progression. Maybe it transcends me into the next step of leadership.

We are all susceptible to failure, and as I'm writing this, my wife is wondering why I don't take a page out of my book in the active listening department. The truth is this is all a lot easier said than done. We all need to be held accountable. Nobody is perfect. I am fortunate enough to have an amazing network of friends and family who hold me to a high standard.

Unfortunately, as I rose in success in my life, I realized that I had a lot of friends who were less than friends and immediately wanted what I had and only wanted me to fail. Sorry, those people have to go.
If someone isn't happy with all of your success, then they aren't your friends. Surround yourself with people you look up to.

As a leader to your peers, you also need to be held accountable for promises made. You are leading, so deliver and deliver as quickly as possible. That sets a precedent for expectations.

Stress

I cannot stress this enough: stress is death. No stress. Find ways to cope with stress. Have hobbies. Breathing techniques. Whatever it takes. I told you I'm going to be straightforward, and the reality is that you might have to work 20-hour days and eat gas station corn dogs and energy drinks. I've lived that lifestyle, and there is a difference between mental and physical stress. I truly believe that mental stress will take a toll on your body quicker than physical stress. Take care of yourself.

Unfortunately, a lot of us don't have the luxury of having a therapist or yoga retreats or whatever it is that de-stresses a person. You need to find that thing I'm telling you. It will catch up with you. If you are already hard on your body, then how do you expect your mind to hold out as long as you do if you are piling stress on it?

The second part of stress is taking on projects and tasks slowly so you can see them to the end and not stress over them at the last minute. You can be your own worst enemy. Set boundaries with yourself. Don't overextend.

I knew a guy who was put into a role that was a little more than he could handle. Had a panic attack in the middle of Sam's Club. He took on way too much and had no way of letting it out. He didn't have a person; he didn't have a stress relief method. He didn't set healthy boundaries. Boom. Collapse. Unfortunately, he had to give up his position, take a pay cut and has since given up on any ambition of moving up in the company. It's unfortunate, but that happens a lot.

Set yourself up for a long, healthy career. That starts with low stress. I find that whenever you are stressed if you yell the word stress, it helps you get some stress out. It signals to the other person that they are causing you stress, and it's funny. It was a lighthearted way I dealt with it, and it has become a running joke among my peers. I think the real solution is to talk to somebody. When on the railroad, you needed to be a manly man, and I think seeing a therapist would be looked down upon, but grow up people. Therapy is awesome. I think that as part of the personal growth journey, it's inevitable. Get the tools for the toolbox that allow you to process stress constructively.

You are responsible TO and not FOR someone else.

Read that again. Cut it out of the page. Put it on your dashboard.

You are not responsible for anyone's decisions or actions. You are responsible to tell them how their actions are affecting you or others. See that stress sliding away?

I've always thought that I could handle tons of stress, and it was a sign of being macho. I never considered the long-term ramifications of butt loads of stress. It finally caught up with me, and after going into A-Fib and being put on heart medication at 35 years old, I started to regret all the stress I put myself through, thinking I was invincible. You are not invincible. It's a silent killer. Take a serious look in the mirror at your family and friends. Nothing is more important than your health. You need to be healthy to work to make a living, so put your health first. Start small. Let's trade those gas station corn dogs for a packed lunch. Let's swap two energy drinks a day for water or a coffee. Take time for yourself and breathe.

Remember that a lot of small transactions equals a large transaction. Find some small things that bring joy; it all adds up. Perhaps you like to read. Anyone can find 10 minutes a day to read. If it helps de-stress, then 10 minutes is better than no minutes.
I'm no expert in this field, so I will let you move on, but It is important, so please take care of yourself.

Face Value

Take me and take others at face value. Tell your team to take you at face value. This is something that I drill into people's heads. Everyone is going to have a bad day. Just take me at face value.

Imagine if you were on the battlefield and you got yelled at to "reload, reload, reload." Then you got your feelers hurt because you were being yelled at. I don't care how I'm being told to do something if my life is in danger. Some people operate that way. I'm sure we all know that old guy that seems like he's mad at everything. He yells when speaking, but he is perfectly happy. Why do you take him at face value but not everyone else? If you can establish this early on about yourself to others, then it won't matter if you're perhaps a little snappy. They will understand that they aren't in trouble or getting fired. You're simply having a bad day.

I asked one of my guys to do something and coughed at the same time I said it. He thought I barked at him and was so stressed the rest of the day that he had to pull me aside that afternoon to make sure I wasn't mad. I didn't even remember what I said. I actually started laughing.

A conversation I have goes like this, "I have bad days just like everyone else in this joint. I am a filter that absorbs the stress of the company, so you don't have to. If I come across as short, please don't take it personally. Just take it at face value. If you think something was directed to you, I would be happy to discuss it and clear the air, but please take what I say for what it is. I will also verbally commit to taking what you say the same way. I understand that things happen in our personal lives, and sometimes the job can be frustrating. Unless you tell me otherwise, I will not read into what you say. Please know that if you are having one of those days and need a shoulder to lean on or would like to talk it through, I'm here for it and can offer a listening ear, or I am happy to help solve problems with you."

This easy conversation has led to many deeper, hard conversations. It has also allowed me to have a stressful day and eliminated some misunderstood buckets of stress thrown on my team. It also lets my team feel like they are empowered to have bad days or personal issues that they can deal with and not get bombarded.

Obviously, if someone is actually going through some major life stress, a simple "are you ok? I'm here if you need me" goes a long way.

Again, this is leadership.

I think the term "get thicker skin" was a rude way of saying what I'm talking about. I've heard that term get thrown around a lot for many reasons. One way I understood it is "Take me at face value, do as I say but pay no attention to how I say it or my body language." Once I made that connection It allowed me to form relationships with people that were really abrasive. I realized that they can't help it. Red in the face, spitting a little bit when they talk, yelling instead of talking, arms flailing around. When really they suffer from high blood pressure, don't have good balance and are deaf, so they have to yell to hear themselves. Once I got past all of that, I made some great friendships. The other thing is you don't know everyone's story. Who knows what anyone is going through. Maybe they see you as intimidating. Or have paralyzing anxiety. Give everyone the benefit of the doubt until they give you a reason or a few reasons to not to.

WHAT DOES IT ALL MEAN?

What does all of this mean at the end of the day?
Well, first off, I'd say it doesn't amount to much if it's not applied.
The point of this field guide is to provide team growth with all of you.
It's personal growth for me to put this on paper. I think that leadership
is a lot of things, and we can dissect it and study it, but nobody has
the answer. Nobody has the perfect formula. You need to do what
works for you, and then you need to tailor that to your peers. You
need to create your own methodology and style. My Grandad used to
tell me as a kid that the smartest people just use more common
sense. That is something I live by. I think that common sense says a
lot of things. You don't need to be a genius to lead. Maybe it's a hard
commodity to find these days? I think that's all leadership is. Just a
little common sense. You don't need me or a book to tell you that,
though.

My sister-in-law is the director of an equine therapy clinic, and she
compared this all to training a horse. You can buy a program, do the
motions, and flip the whip, but really, it's about forming a relationship
with that animal. Eventually, that animal will look out for your best
interest. You've optimized the ability to trust and vice versa through
proper leadership.

That this is the ultimate goal. Leadership is a lot of work. You become
a therapist. The person with all the answers. It's not for everybody. I
have had a conversation with a manager who admitted, "I don't want
to hear about everyone's problems, I just want to tell them what to do."
Fine. You can do that. Don't expect your team to win any awards.
Don't expect a promotion. Unless you're so
deeply rooted in nepotism that you have a free ticket up. In that case,
enjoy the ride because everyone is going to hate you anyway.

If I were to summarize this all into one word, it would simply be
Integrity. That is the secret sauce. Sorry, I made you read to the end
to get here, but what else could leadership be?

What's Next?

Alright, what's next? You've gone through my guide, tried everything, but still find it tough? That's actually a good sign. Have you ever heard of the Dunning-Kruger effect? It's when we first think we know all there is about something. But the more we learn or practice, the more we realize how much we don't know. Even though it feels like we're not getting anywhere, we're actually getting better at it, probably more than most people. It's all part of the journey.

You're serious about leadership, it's obvious or you wouldn't have made it this far. Start with yourself.
How can I be a better human?
What are my strengths and weaknesses?
How can I contribute in a meaningful way?
Do I have integrity?
Start with bite-size goals. Like any skill, leadership is like learning the guitar. It takes time, effort and practice.

Start with attitude. A bite-size goal that you can chew on. Let's get that part out of the way, and then we can work on some effective communication. All the while, we are reducing stress, homing in on personal growth and some accountability. Then, let's add some optimization. A little spice, something nice.... Get forklift certified, and now you have unlocked the secret to life.

As your tour guide through leadership, I'm going to leave you with a cheat sheet and do the hard work for you. It's been fun, thanks for hanging out.

PS. These make great meeting topics.

FIELD GUIDE CHEAT SHEET

1. Mastering Communication in the Field:

- Focus on Documentation: Keep records of everything. It's your blueprint for success.
- Listen More, Speak Less: Your ears are your greatest tools. Understand before being understood.
- Find Common Ground: Discover shared experiences and goals to strengthen team bonds.

2. The Right Attitude on the Job:

- Lead by Example: No task is too small for any leader.
- Supportive Collaboration: I'm here to help, let's solve problems together.
- Team Spirit: Remember, it's always 'we', never 'I'.
- Shift Your Perspective: View challenges as opportunities for growth and innovation.

3. Getting the Best from Your Team:

- Set Clear Expectations: Everyone should know what's expected of them.
- Adapt and Evolve: Goals may change; flexibility is key.
- Equip for Success: Provide the tools and support.
- Lead with Kindness: Respect and empathy go a long way

4. From Leader to Mentor:

- Invest in Relationships: Take someone under your wing.
- Be a bridge, Not a Gatekeeper: Facilitate opportunities; don't restrict them.

- Mentorship vs. Manipulation: Always maintain integrity and transparent intentions.
- Establish Healthy Boundaries: Professional yet caring.

5. Navigating the Leadership Journey:

- Focus on Personal Growth: Invest in your development as you lead.
- Foster Team Development: Grow together, celebrating collective victories.
- Uphold Accountability: Be responsible for actions and decisions, yours and the team's.
- Manage Stress Effectively: Keep a cool head in challenging times.
- Value Authentic Interactions: Engage with honesty and transparency.

References

Allport, Gordon W. *Personality: A Psychological Interpretation*. New York: Henry Holt and Company, 1937.

Dunning, D., & Kruger, J. (1999). Unskilled and unaware of it: How difficulties in recognizing one's own incompetence lead to inflated self-assessments. *Journal of Personality and Social Psychology*, 77(6), 1121-1134.

Dweck, C. S. (2006). *Mindset: The New Psychology of Success*. Random House.

Greenleaf, R. K. (1970). The Servant as Leader. *Robert K. Greenleaf Center*.

Geller, E. S. (n.d.). Actively Caring for People: Cultivating a Culture of Compassion. *Virginia Tech*.

NOTES